Maria,
Love Jesus,
Love His Church!
Sharon [illegible]

We Have A Pope!

KAREN CONGENI

NEW SPRINGTIME PRESS
AKRON, OHIO

To my parents, Dave and Shirley Clark

PUBLISHED BY NEW SPRINGTIME PRESS
www.newspringtimepress.com

Art direction: Steve Tomasko
Cover and interior design: Leslie Seibert
Editorial credits: Laura Brestovansky; Mary Harwell Sayler
Photo credits: Creative Commons, 17; David Q. Hall, 6; © Fotosearch, 10; Francesca Congeni, 7; Leslie Seibert, 8; © Pavel Mitrofanov/Fotolia, 11; © Photographic Service L'O.R., front cover, 5, 14, 15, 16, 18-29, back cover, back flap; Public Domain, 9, 12

Scripture verses are from the Catholic Edition of the Revised Standard Version of the Bible produced by the National Council of Churches of Christ in the United States of America.

List of popes courtesy of Catholic Answers. www.catholic.com

Nihil Obstat: Sister Mary McCormick, OSU, Ph.D.
Censor Deputatus

Imprimatur: The Most Reverend Richard G. Lennon, M.Th., M.A.
Bishop of Cleveland
Given at Cleveland, Ohio, on 28 October 2009

The *Nihil Obstat* and *Imprimatur* are official declarations that a book or pamphlet is free of doctrinal or moral error. No implication is contained therein that those who have granted the *Nihil Obstat* and *Imprimatur* agree with the contents, opinions, or statements expressed.

ISBN 978-0-9825376-0-2

Printed in Singapore
FIRST EDITION
10 9 8 7 6 5 4 3 2 1

He said to them, "But who do you say that I am?"

Simon Peter replied, "You are the Christ, the Son of the living God."

And Jesus answered him, "Blessed are you, Simon Bar-Jona! For flesh and blood has not revealed this to you, but my Father who is in heaven. And I tell you, you are Peter, and on this rock I will build my church, and the powers of death shall not prevail against it. I will give you the keys of the kingdom of heaven, and whatever you bind on earth shall be bound in heaven, and whatever you loose on earth shall be loosed in heaven."

Matthew 16:15-19 (RSV-Catholic).

Pope means Papa.
The pope is our Holy Father.
He is the leader of the Catholic Church.

Many years ago, Jesus said to a fisherman named Simon, “You have been catching fish. Now you will catch people for God.” Jesus gave Simon a new name: Peter.

Peter means rock—strong, solid rock.
"On this rock I will build my Church," Jesus said.

Jesus had a special plan for Peter.
Jesus needed someone to teach many people.
He needed someone to lead His Church.

Jesus gave the keys of the kingdom of Heaven
to Peter. Jesus let Peter lead the Church.
Peter became our first pope.

“Take care of my sheep,” Jesus told Peter. As a shepherd protects sheep, Peter would protect God’s people.

Jesus promised to send the Holy Spirit to help Peter.

Peter led God's people. He taught them about the love of Jesus. He taught them to love one another. He healed them.

The Bible names Peter more times than all of the other apostles put together. In a list of apostles, Peter is named first. Sometimes this group of Jesus' friends is called "Peter and the Twelve."

Peter loved Jesus so much he was willing to die for Jesus. And he did.

When Peter died, another pope began to shepherd God's people. After him came another pope and then another, and on and on until today.

Jesus taught His followers many things. The pope also teaches the followers of Jesus. The Holy Spirit helps each pope.

In two thousand years, many popes have led the people, but God stays the same. So do His teachings.

When Jesus asked Peter to lead the Church, He gave him a new name. Today each new pope gets a new name too.

Joseph Ratzinger took the name Benedict. Fifteen popes had that name before him. So he became Pope Benedict XVI.

The pope lives in Vatican City. Even though the Vatican is called a city, it is really a country—the smallest country in the world. Vatican City is in Rome, Italy.

Jesus and Peter walked from place to place.
Now the pope can ride in the Popemobile.

A colorful army, the Swiss Guard, protects the pope.

The pope wears a gold ring with a picture of a fisherman in honor of our first pope, Peter. When a pope dies, someone slips the ring from his finger. A silver hammer crushes the ring.

People feel crushed too! They mourn for nine days. They pray. They go to a special Mass for the pope.

Cardinals come to the Vatican from around the world. The cardinals ask God to help them pick the best leader. They talk. They pray. They listen. Then they vote.

In Saint Peter's Square, thousands of people wait and pray.

Smoke rises from the chimney of the Sistine Chapel.
If the smoke is black, a pope has not yet been chosen.

When a pope is chosen, white smoke rises.

"*Habemus papam!*" someone shouts.
We have a pope!

Bells ring! The people clap and cheer. They thank God for choosing a new pope to lead the Church.

The new pope blesses everyone.

Happily, the people shout, "*Viva il Papa!*"

Long live the pope!

Glossary:

Apostles—Twelve followers of Jesus chosen by Him to spread the Good News of Jesus Christ

Basilica—A Roman Catholic church with special privileges given by the pope

Cardinal—A special priest who wears red like a cardinal bird; When a pope has died, cardinals vote for the new pope.

Habemus papam—Latin for "We have a pope." Latin is the official language of the Roman Catholic Church.

Holy Spirit—The third Person of the Trinity; The Holy Spirit is the Author and Interpreter of Scripture. The Holy Spirit guides the pope. The Holy Spirit also guides the bishops when they act as one with the pope.

Keys—Tools used to unlock something; Peter was given the keys to Heaven. This means he was given permission to guide the Church and in this way, lead God's people to Heaven.

Mourn—To have deep sadness

Prince of the Apostles—A title for Saint Peter

Ring of the Fisherman—A ring worn by the pope with a picture of Saint Peter; In years past, the pope used it to stamp important papers written for the Church. When the pope died, the ring was destroyed so that no one else could use it for this purpose.

Saint Peter's Basilica—A major basilica in the Vatican; The main altar is built over the place where Saint Peter is buried.

Saint Peter's Square—The open space in front of Saint Peter's Basilica

Sistine Chapel—A chapel in the Apostolic Palace at the Vatican

Staff—A strong, straight stick with a hook at one end; A shepherd uses it to poke or pull a lost sheep back to the safety of the flock. The pope carries a staff or Papal Cross.

Viva il Papa—Italian for "Long live the pope." The language of Italy is Italian.

XVI—Roman numerals for the number sixteen; Joseph Cardinal Ratzinger became Pope Benedict XVI.

Saint Peter was the first pope,
then came Linus,
then…

…Anacletus, Clement, Evaristus, Alexander I, Sixtus I, Telesphorus, Hyginus, Pius I, Anicetus, Soter, Eleutherius, Victor I, Zephyrinus, Callistus I, Urban I, Pontian, Anterus, Fabian, Cornelius, Lucius I, Stephen I, Sixtus II, Dionysius, Felix I, Eutychian, Caius, Marcellinus, Marcellus I, Eusebius, Miltiades, Sylvester I, Marcus, Julius I, Liberius, Damasus I, Siricius, Anastasius I, Innocent I, Zosimus, Boniface I, Celestine I, Sixtus III, Leo I the Great, Hilarius, Simplicius, Felix II, Gelasius I, Anastasius II, Symmachus, Hormisdas, John I, Felix III, Boniface II, John II, Agapitus I, Silverius, Vigilius, Pelagius I, John III, Benedict I, Pelagius II, Gregory I the Great, Sabinian, Boniface III, Boniface IV, Adeodatus I, Boniface V, Honorius I, Severinus, John IV, Theodore I, Martin I, Eugene I, Vitalian, Adeodatus II, Donus, Agatho, Leo II, Benedict II, John V, Conon, Sergius I, John VI, John VII, Sisinnius, Constantine, Gregory II, Gregory III, Zachary, Stephen II, Stephen III, Paul I, Stephen IV, Adrian I, Leo III, Stephen V, Paschal I, Eugene II, Valentine, Gregory IV, Sergius II, Leo IV, Benedict III, Nicholas I the Great, Adrian II, John VIII, Marinus I, Adrian III, Stephen VI, Formosus, Boniface VI, Stephen VII, Romanus, Theodore II, John IX, Benedict IV, Leo V, Sergius III, Anastasius III, Lando, John X, Leo VI, Stephen VIII, John XI, Leo VII, Stephen IX, Marinus II, Agapetus II, John XII, Leo VIII, Benedict V, John XIII, Benedict VI, Benedict VII, John XIV, John XV, Gregory V, Sylvester II, John XVII, John XVIII, Sergius IV, Benedict VIII, John XIX, Benedict IX, Sylvester III, Benedict IX, Gregory VI, Clement II, Benedict IX, Damasus II, Leo IX, Victor II, Stephen X, Nicholas II, Alexander II, Gregory VII, Victor III, Urban II, Paschal II, Gelasius II, Callistus II, Honorius II, Innocent II, Celestine II, Lucius II, Eugene III, Anastasius IV, Adrian IV, Alexander III, Lucius III, Urban III, Gregory VIII, Clement III, Celestine III, Innocent III, Honorius III, Gregory IX, Celestine IV, Innocent IV, Alexander IV, Urban IV, Clement IV, Gregory X, Innocent V, Adrian V, John XXI, Nicholas III, Martin IV, Honorius IV, Nicholas IV, Celestine V, Boniface VIII, Benedict XI, Clement V, John XXII, Benedict XII, Clement VI, Innocent VI, Urban V, Gregory XI, Urban VI, Boniface IX, Innocent VII, Gregory XII, Martin V, Eugene IV, Nicholas V, Callistus III, Pius II, Paul II, Sixtus IV, Innocent VIII, Alexander VI, Pius III, Julius II, Leo X, Adrian VI, Clement VII, Paul III, Julius III, Marcellus II, Paul IV, Pius IV, Pius V, Gregory XIII, Sixtus V, Urban VII, Gregory XIV, Innocent IX, Clement VIII, Leo XI, Paul V, Gregory XV, Urban VIII, Innocent X, Alexander VII, Clement IX, Clement X, Innocent XI, Alexander VIII, Innocent XII, Clement XI, Innocent XIII, Benedict XIII, Clement XII, Benedict XIV, Clement XIII, Clement XIV, Pius VI, Pius VII, Leo XII, Pius VIII, Gregory XVI, Pius IX, Leo XIII, Pius X, Benedict XV, Pius XI, Pius XII, John XXIII, Paul VI, John Paul I, John Paul II, Benedict XVI

When they had finished breakfast, Jesus said to Simon Peter, "Simon, son of John, do you love me more than these?" He said to him, "Yes, Lord; you know that I love you." He said to him, "Feed my lambs."

A second time he said to him, "Simon, son of John, do you love me?" He said to him, "Yes, Lord; you know that I love you." He said to him, "Tend my sheep."

He said to him the third time, "Simon, son of John, do you love me?" Peter was grieved because he said to him the third time, "Do you love me?" And he said to him, "Lord, you know everything; you know that I love you." Jesus said to him, "Feed my sheep."

John 21:15-17 (RSV-Catholic).